The family thigh problem begins with the mouth.

by Cathy Guisewite

Selected Cartoons from
MY GRANDDAUGHTER HAS FLEAS!

FAWCETT CREST • NEW YORK

Cathy © is syndicated internationally by Universal Press Syndicate

A Fawcett Crest Book
Published by Ballantine Books
Copyright © 1989 by Universal Press Syndicate

Library of Congress Catalog Card Number: 89-84809

ISBN 0-449-21916-X

This book comprises a portion of MY GRANDDAUGHTER HAS FLEAS! and
is reprinted by arrangement with Andrews and McMeel, a Universal Press
Syndicate Company.

Manufactured in the United States of America

First Ballantine Books Edition: November 1990

MOM AND FLO! I THOUGHT YOU TWO WENT OUT OF THE BODY-BUILDING BUSINESS.

OUT? NO!

WE JUST REALIZED THAT HAVING A TRIM, TONED BODY IS MEANINGLESS IF YOUR CHOLESTEROL COUNT IS TOO HIGH.

THUS, FLO WILL CONDUCT A GRUELING WORKOUT, AFTER WHICH I WILL FEED YOU A BIG PLATE OF OATBRAN MUFFINS!

A SIMPLE MATTER OF BROADENING OUR CLIENT'S BASES!!

BROADENING OUR BASE OF CLIENTS.

WHATEVER.

SOME WOMEN SHOP EVERY DAY, CONSTANTLY REFINING THEIR OWN TASTES AND NEEDS AS THEY SCRUTINIZE WHAT'S AVAILABLE.

SOME WOMEN HAVE A FINE WARDROBE INTACT, AND GO OUT ONCE PER SEASON TO SELECT ACCESSORIES TO UPDATE THEIR ORIGINAL INVESTMENT.

SOME WAIT UNTIL THEY'RE DESPERATE AND THEN FLING THEMSELVES ONTO THE MERCY OF A SALESPERSON WHO WILL TALK THEM INTO TRYING SOMETHING, WHETHER OR NOT IT HAS ANYTHING TO DO WITH THEIR LIVES.

THE BLIND DATE APPROACH TO GETTING DRESSED.

IT'S YOU.

SEE HOW FEMININE THE WIDE PLAID TROUSERS BECOME WITH A TOUCH OF MAGENTA AT THE NECK ?

SEE HOW THE 10 YARDS OF FABRIC FLOW OVER YOU, EVER SO SUBTLY OUTLINING YOUR CURVACEOUS, FEMININE LEGS ?

SEE HOW THEY SEEM TO SAY, "I'M SO FEMININE, I CAN DRESS LIKE MY UNCLE RALPH AND STILL EXUDE WOMANLY CHARMS" ??!

HAH.

SEE WHY FALL '88 IS MAKING MORE AND MORE SALESPEOPLE START LOOKING FOR NEW CAREERS ?

WOMEN WANTED TO BE SEXIER... ...THEN REJECTED THE MINI-SKIRT AS TOO "TRAMPY." YOU WANTED TO BE MORE PROFES-SIONAL...THEN REJECTED THE BUSINESS SUIT AS TOO "STUFFY."

YOU WANTED TO BE MORE FEMI-NINE... THEN REJECTED THE BUBBLE DRESS AS TOO "CUTESY." FINE. WE GIVE UP.

EVERY CONCEIVABLE SHAPE, SIZE AND LENGTH IS HERE THIS YEAR. YOU'RE ON YOUR OWN! WE'RE SICK OF HEARING WHAT WOM-EN WANT ONLY TO HAVE YOU POOH-POOH IT AFTER WE KILL OUR-SELVES TRYING TO PROVIDE IT!

YES! BRAVO! WELL PUT!!

NOW, MORE THAN EVER, LEAVE YOUR MALE FRIENDS AT HOME WHEN YOU GO SHOPPING.

WE'VE WATCHED THE CANDIDATES IN ACTION... SEEN THEIR VIDEOS.. ..HEARD THEIR SOUND BITES... READ THEIR CLAIMS... ARGUED WITH OUR FRIENDS...

AND NOW, IN THE RICHEST TRA- DITION OF AMERICA, WE NEED EACH TO SIT ALONE, GATHER THE INFORMATION AROUND US...

...AND EVER SO CALMLY AND QUIETLY BEGIN TO ASK OURSELVES THE QUESTION WE ASK AT LEAST ONCE EVERY FOUR YEARS....

IS THERE STILL HOPE FOR LIFE ON MARS?

SENATE REPUBLICANS KILLED A DAY CARE SUBSIDY PLAN THIS MONTH, PREFERRING TO BACK BUSH'S PLAN TO GIVE FAMILIES A $1,000 TAX CREDIT FOR EACH CHILD UNDER AGE 4.

THE BUSH PLAN COMES TO $2.74 PER DAY PER CHILD. WHILE NO ONE COULD FIND DECENT DAY CARE FOR $2.74 A DAY, HIS PLAN WOULD ALLOW EACH IMPOVERISHED FAMILY TO BUY A DECENT VCR.

NOT ONLY WOULD CHILDREN HAVE SOMETHING TO WATCH WHILE MOMMY RIPS HER HAIR OUT, BUT EACH VCR PURCHASE WOULD FURTHER BOOST THE JAPANESE ECONOMY SO THEY COULD KEEP BOOSTING OUR ECONOMY BY BUYING UP ALL OUR BUILDINGS AND BUSINESSES.

PARENTS, OF COURSE, COULD TAPE ALL SPEECHES EXPLAINING HOW WELL OFF WE ARE.

GET YOUR BOTTLE, HONEY. MOMMY HAS TO GO TO BED FOR FOUR YEARS.

THE REAGAN-BUSH ADMINIS-
TRATION HAS DONE NOTHING
ABOUT THE FACT THAT 44%
OF THE WORK FORCE IS WOM-
EN, BUT WE STILL HAVE NO
NATIONAL LAW REQUIRING
EQUAL PAY.

IT'S DONE NOTHING ABOUT THE
FACT THAT 67% OF THE WOM-
EN WHO HAVE PRESCHOOL CHIL-
DREN WORK FULL TIME AND
NEED DAY CARE HELP... NOTHING
ABOUT THE FACT THAT ALMOST
90% OF THE FAMILIES ON
WELFARE ARE SINGLE MOTHERS
WITH NO WAY OUT.

YET, INCREDIBLY, MANY PEOPLE
LOOK AT THE CURRENT GOV-
ERNMENT AND THINK THINGS
ARE GOING PRETTY WELL.

THE GOVERNMENT IS LIKE A
BABY. IT LOOKS LIKE A LITTLE
ANGEL WHEN IT'S SLEEPING.

BY NOV. 8, $65 MILLION WILL HAVE BEEN SPENT IN THE PRESIDENTIAL RACE. BECAUSE OF THE GOVERNMENT'S FUND-MATCHING PROGRAM, APPROXIMATELY ONE-FOURTH OF THAT WILL HAVE BEEN FROM OUR OWN INCOME TAX DOLLARS.

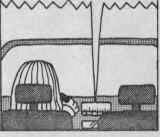

CANDIDATES WILL HAVE SPENT $16 MILLION OF OUR OWN HARD-EARNED MONEY TRYING TO CONVINCE US THEY'RE MOST QUALIFIED TO MANAGE THE FINANCES OF THE COUNTRY...

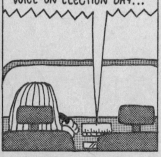

WHILE THE RESULT IS STILL SPECULATION, THERE'S A GROWING FEELING THAT WE'LL BE HEARING ONE STRONG, UNIFIED VOICE ON ELECTION DAY...

I WANT A REFUND!!!

LOOK WHAT MOMMY WROTE, ZENITH... "25% OF THE CHILDREN IN THE COUNTRY TODAY LIVE WITH A SINGLE PARENT. WE NEED DUKAKIS BECAUSE HE SUPPORTS A NATIONAL DAY-CARE PLAN AND LAWS TO RAISE DAY-CARE STANDARDS."

"44% OF THE WORKFORCE ARE WOMEN, BUT WOMEN EARN ONLY 64% OF WHAT MEN DO. WE NEED DUKAKIS BECAUSE HE SUPPORTS LAWS FOR EQUAL PAY."

"80% OF THE WOMEN WILL GET PREGNANT DURING THEIR WORKING LIVES. WE NEED DUKAKIS BECAUSE HE SUPPORTS JOB-PROTECTED MATERNITY LEAVES."

SPLOOSH!

...AND 99% OF ALL CHILDREN UNDER AGE 3 WILL STUFF POLITICAL FLIERS DOWN THE TOILET BEFORE MOMMY HAS A CHANCE TO HAND THEM OUT.

SINCE 1981, AID TO EDUCATION HAS BEEN CUT BY 16%... FUNDS FOR WATER POLLUTION CONTROL HAVE BEEN CUT BY 43%... CHILD-CARE FUNDING HAS BEEN CUT BY 28%... THE MINIMUM WAGE HAS DROPPED IN REAL VALUE BY 31%...

ANDREA, THERE'S NOTHING AS ANNOYING AS SOMEONE WHO'S STOPPED BY THE DEMOCRATIC HEADQUARTERS AND PICKED UP A BUNCH OF THEIR STATISTICS.

IF YOU WANT TO TALK POLITICS, COME BACK WHEN YOU HAVE FAIR, NON-PARTISAN, NON-SUBJECTIVE FACTS.

DING DONG!

FOUR OUT OF THE LAST 10 VICE PRESIDENTS BECAME PRESIDENT.

WHEN REPUBLICANS TALK ABOUT THE THRIVING ECONOMY THEY'VE BUILT, THEY DON'T MENTION THAT THEIR ECONOMY REQUIRES MOST MOTHERS TO WORK OUTSIDE THE HOME TO TRY TO HELP PAY THE BILLS.

WHEN THEY TALK ABOUT FAMILY VALUES, THEY DON'T MENTION THAT THEY'VE CONSISTENTLY VOTED AGAINST ANY LEGISLATION THAT WOULD HELP STRUGGLING WORKING MOTHERS OUT OF THE HOLE.

WHEN WOMEN HAVE NO CHOICE BUT TO WORK MORE AND SPEND LESS TIME WITH THEIR CHILDREN, WHAT DO REPUBLICANS THINK ALL THOSE CHILDREN ARE GOING TO DO?!

CHILDREN WILL DO WHAT THEY'VE ALWAYS DONE, ANDREA.

GROW UP AND BLAME THEIR MOTHERS.

IN A STARTLING ELECTION POLL REVERSAL, 93% OF ALL AMERICAN VOTERS NOW REPORT BEING MIFFED THAT NO ONE EVER CALLS THEM WHEN THEY'RE CONDUCTING POLLS.

THIS IS UP FROM LAST WEEK'S POLL, WHICH SHOWED THAT 52% WOULD RATHER LISTEN TO POLLS THAN WATCH THE NEW FALL TV SEASON.

WHILE 37% THINK THE POLLS ARE THE NEW FALL TV SEASON, THE 76% WHO FORMERLY SAID THEY IGNORE POLLS ARE NOW DIVIDED AMONG 8% WHO LIKE POLLS, 27% WHO MAKE UP THEIR OWN POLLS, AND 41% WHO SAY THEY'LL VOTE AGAINST POLLS JUST TO PUT THEM OUT OF BUSINESS.

AND NOW LET'S HEAR WHAT THE CANDIDATES ARE SAYING IN THESE CRITICAL LAST DAYS BEFORE THE ELECTION...

OOPS. SORRY. WE'RE OUT OF TIME, JOHN...

CLICK!

IN THE GREAT AMERICAN
TRADITION OF INDEPENDENCE,
WE EACH HAVE OUR OWN
IDEAS ABOUT WHAT'S BEST
FOR THE COUNTRY.

IN THE GREAT AMERICAN
TRADITION OF DEMOCRACY, WE
CAST OUR VOTES FOR THE
PEOPLE WE FIRMLY BELIEVE
WILL ENSURE A PROSPEROUS,
PEACEFUL, PRODUCTIVE, HAPPY
FUTURE FOR OURSELVES AND
OUR LOVED ONES.

IN THE GREAT AMERICAN TRA-
DITION OF HEDGING OUR BETS,
WE STOP ON THE WAY HOME
AND BUY A LOTTERY TICKET.

HOW'S THANKS-GIVING DINNER COMING?

WONDERFUL! I LET CATHY STEW OVER MY CRITIQUE OF HER HAIR WHILE I GRILLED HER ABOUT HER FUTURE WITH IRVING!

JUST AS SHE REACHED THE BOILING POINT, I SPRINKLED IN SOME COMMENTS ABOUT HOW SHE'S RAISING HER PUPPY.

I'M LETTING THAT SIMMER FOR ABOUT 20 MINUTES......THEN I'LL CHOP UP HER DE- FENSE OF HER CAREER PATH......TOSS IN SOME FREE ADVICE ABOUT HER WARDROBE...AND LET THE WHOLE WORKS FRY!!

IS ANY ACTUAL FOOD BEING PRE- PARED IN HERE?

WHO HAS TIME FOR FOOD?

MAY I COME IN THE KITCH-EN YET, CATHY?

NO, YOU MAY NOT COME IN YET!

WHAT ARE YOU DOING IN THERE?

IRVING, I HAVE CATALOGS TO GO THROUGH...GIFTS TO FIGURE OUT...CARDS TO ADDRESS...LISTS TO MAKE...

CHRISTMAS IS LESS THAN FOUR WEEKS AWAY! I'M DOING WHAT EVERY WOMAN IN THE COUNTRY IS DOING TONIGHT!!!

HOW OPRAH LOST THE WEIGHT

FRANKIE DOESN'T CALL BECAUSE HE'S AFRAID I'LL GET HURT... I WON'T CALL ANYONE BEFORE I'M RECOVERED FROM FRANKIE BECAUSE I'M AFRAID THE NEW PERSON WOULD GET HURT...

EVEN IF I WERE RECOVERED FROM FRANKIE, I WOULDN'T CALL ANYONE NEW BECAUSE I MIGHT CHANGE MY MIND AND HE'D GET HURT...IF FRANKIE THOUGHT I WAS EVEN THINKING OF SOMEONE NEW, HE'D GET HURT...

IF I DON'T TRY TO MEET ANYONE, I MIGHT GET HURT...BUT IF I GET HURT, I WILL DEFINITELY GO MEET SOMEONE AND THEN HE WOULD GET HURT, I WOULD GET HURT AND FRANKIE WOULD GET HURT.

NO ONE ACTUALLY DATES ANYMORE, CHARLENE. WE'RE ALL JUST PROTECTING EACH OTHER.

"OH, DARLING," HE'LL SAY, "I'LL CARRY IT ALWAYS AND THINK OF YOU".... HE'LL CARRY IT ON HIS NEXT BUSINESS TRIP AND THINK OF ME.....

FINE ITALIAN ATTACHES

THE WOMAN NEXT TO HIM ON THE PLANE WILL BE IMPRESSED BY ITS INCREDIBLE STYLE... THEY'LL CHAT AND LAUGH...HE'LL START POSTPONING HIS TRIP HOME... HIS CALLS WILL STOP... THE OPERATOR WON'T LET ME THROUGH TO HIS ROOM ANYMORE...

AAACK!!

CATHY! WHAT HAPPENED ??

SOMEWHERE BETWEEN THE DISPLAY AREA AND THE CASHIER, MY ROMANTIC FANTASY QUIT HAVING ME IN IT.

THIS SWEATER IS PERFECT!

IRVING WOULDN'T WEAR A SWEATER LIKE THAT.

BUT HE'D LOOK SO GREAT IN IT!

CATHY, NEVER GIVE A MAN SOMETHING THAT MATCHES YOUR TASTE INSTEAD OF HIS!

IT SAYS YOU'RE TRYING TO TRANSFORM HIM...YOU'RE CRITICAL OF HIS USUAL STYLE...INSENSITIVE TO HOW UNCOMFORTABLE HE'D BE ABOUT HAVING TO WEAR SOMETHING YOU GAVE HIM...AND TOTALLY OBLIVIOUS TO HIS OWN SENSE OF HIMSELF!

THAT WILL BE $88.95.

THEN AGAIN, HOW OFTEN DO YOU COME ACROSS A GIFT WITH THIS MUCH MEANING?

"DURING THE FRANTIC HOLIDAY SEASON, IT'S IMPORTANT TO TAKE TIME TO PAMPER YOUR OVEREXERTED SENSES..."

"INVEST IN A SOOTHING, HOUR-LONG PROFESSIONAL MASSAGE... THEN HAVE A LONG, LUXURIOUS BUBBLE BATH, TAKING TIME TO REJUVENATE TIRED SKIN WITH A GENTLE LOOFAH RUB..."

"RESTORE INNER HARMONY WITH 45 MINUTES OF MEDITATIVE MUSIC AND YOGA STRETCHES... FOLLOW WITH A 30-MINUTE RE-VITALIZING YOGURT MASK... A HOT OIL TREATMENT... FRESH MANICURE IN A PERKY HOLIDAY COLOR... AND HOP INTO BED WITH A PIPING MUG OF HERBAL TEA."

...OR SAVE 5½ HOURS BY THROWING OUT THE MAGAZINE AND EATING A BOWL OF POPCORN.

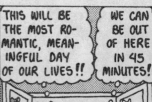

MY LEFT BRAIN IS MAKING LISTS OF PEOPLE I HAVEN'T SENT CARDS TO YET... MY RIGHT BRAIN IS AT THE CRAFT STORE, THINKING UP CREATIVE GIFTS I COULD STILL MAKE BEFORE SUNDAY...

MY NERVES ARE AT THE MALL, WORRYING WHETHER I SHOULD HAVE GOTTEN THE OTHER NECKTIE FOR DAD... MY STOMACH IS STILL AT LAST NIGHT'S PARTY, BEGGING FOR MORE CHRISTMAS COOKIES...

...AND MY HEART IS STUCK IN TRAFFIC SOMEWHERE BETWEEN MY MOTHER'S HOUSE, MY BOYFRIEND'S HOUSE AND THE ADORABLE MAN I SAW AT THE POST OFFICE.

WHAT IS IT YOU WANT, CATHY?

MAY WHAT'S LEFT OF ME SNEAK HOME EARLY AND TAKE A NAP?

I ACCEPTED IRVING'S INVITATION TO THIS PARTY WITHOUT GRILLING HIM ABOUT WHAT I WAS SUPPOSED TO WEAR.

I DIDN'T ASK WHAT HE WAS WEARING...I DIDN'T MAKE HIM CALL THE HOST...I DIDN'T FORCE HIM TO SNEAK OVER TO THE PARTY EARLY AND PEEK IN THE WINDOW....

FOR ONCE IN MY LIFE, I AM WALKING INTO A SITUATION EXUDING CONFIDENCE AND NONCHALANCE!!

HI! I HAVE TO GO HOME AND CHANGE CLOTHES.

I KNEW IT WAS TOO GOOD TO BE TRUE.

MOST SHOPPERS MAKE THEIR CHRISTMAS RETURNS THE DAY AFTER CHRISTMAS. IT'S A BIG HELP TO THE STORE OWNERS.

SOME WAIT UNTIL THE FIRST WEEK OF THE NEW YEAR SO THEY CAN CASH IN ON THE HOTTEST SALES.

THIS WEEK, AS WE CELEBRATE THE ONE-MONTH ANNIVERSARY OF CHRISTMAS, WE SEE THOSE SPECIAL INDIVIDUALS WHO ARE MOTIVATED BY SOMETHING EVEN LARGER THAN ALTRUISM AND GOOD BARGAINS....

...THE ONES WHO JUST GOT THEIR CHARGE CARD STATEMENTS FOR DECEMBER.

I TRIED THIS DRESS ON AT THE STORE FIVE TIMES ON THREE SEPARATE DAYS IN EARLY DECEMBER.

I BROUGHT IT HOME, TRIED IT ON 22 MORE TIMES DURING THE NEXT SIX WEEKS, AND SPENT A WHOLE EVENING MODELING IT WITH EVERYTHING IN MY CLOSET.

ALTHOUGH I'VE HAD THE DRESS ON 27 TIMES, PAID FOR IT, AND SHOWN IT TO EVERYONE I KNOW, IT HAS NOT TECHNICALLY BEEN "WORN," AND COULD BE RETURNED.

EVERYONE THINKS WE'RE MARRIED AND I'M STILL TRYING TO DECIDE WHETHER OR NOT I WANT TO GO OUT.

THE SALESWOMAN SPENT 45 MINUTES HELPING ME WHILE I AGONIZED OVER WHETHER TO GET THIS DRESS...

SHE COMPLIMENTED ME, ENCOURAGED ME, AND CHEERFULLY HUNG UP THE 17 OTHER OUTFITS I HAD TO TRY ON BEFORE I COULD MAKE A DECISION.

NOW I'M DRIVING 30 MILES OUT OF MY WAY SO I CAN RETURN IT AT A DIFFERENT BRANCH OF THE STORE SO I WON'T HAVE TO SEE HER FACE.

THERE'S NO LIMIT TO HOW FAR WE'LL GO TO AVOID SOMEONE WHO'S BEEN GOOD TO US.

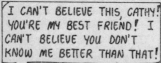

DELIRIOUS WITH FEVER, SHE STAGGERS INTO THE BATHROOM AND PUTS ON EYELINER JUST IN CASE HER SWEETHEART DECIDES TO STOP OVER WITH SOME NICE, HOT SOUP...

HEAD THROBBING, STOMACH REELING, LUNGS CRACKING, SHE MANAGES TO TRY ON EVERY NIGHTGOWN UNTIL SHE FINDS THE MOST FLATTERING, JUST IN CASE HER SWEETIE DECIDES TO SURPRISE HER WITH SOME GET-WELL FLOWERS...

...IRVING??

WILL YOU CALL MY DOCTOR, CATHY? I HAVE A LITTLE SORE THROAT.

MUSCLES ACHING, SHE SOME- HOW FINDS THE STRENGTH TO REARRANGE HER PHOTO ALBUM OF HER LOVED ONE....

BLEAH!

MY MOTHER, A SELF-SACRIFICING HOUSEWIFE, NEVER LET HAVING THE FLU COME BEFORE THE NEEDS OF HER FAMILY.

I'M WEARING AN OXYGEN MASK SO I WON'T GET GERMS ON THE BREAD I'M BAKING.

I, A DYNAMIC CAREER WOMAN, FLOP INTO BED AND LEAVE PATHETIC MESSAGES ON ALL MY FRIENDS' ANSWERING MACHINES AT THE FIRST SIGN OF A SNIFFLE.

THAT'S THE DIFFERENCE BETWEEN OUR GENERATIONS...

WOMEN TODAY HAVE SO MUCH MORE SELF-RESPECT.

I'M SICK. I CAN'T BREATHE! FAX ME SOME SOUP!

WOMEN TODAY SEE THE VALENTINE INDUSTRY FOR THE COMMERCIALIZED HYPE THAT IT IS.

GET REAL.

WE DO NOT MEASURE OUR SELF-WORTH BY WHETHER OR NOT WE GET A VALENTINE.

WHO DESIGNS THIS? WHO DO THEY THINK WANTS THIS??

IN FACT, FOR MANY WOMEN, ONLY ONE OTHER EVENT ALL YEAR INSPIRES SUCH FEELINGS OF TOTAL, UTTER INDIGNATION.

VALENTINE'S DAY: BATHING SUIT SEASON FOR THE HEART.

AND WHERE'S THE ONE FOR ME??!

MY WORST WAS THE VALENTINE'S DAY I SPENT $200 ON LINGERIE... WAS TOO EMBARRASSED TO LET MY DATE IN THE FRONT DOOR... AND THEN SULKED FOR A MONTH BECAUSE HE DIDN'T RESPOND TO THE SEDUCTION HE NEVER KNEW I WAS TRYING...

I ONCE BAKED A VALENTINE CAKE FOR MY DATE... GOT NERVOUS... ATE THE WHOLE THING BEFORE HE GOT THERE AND THEN WOULDN'T LET HIM TOUCH ME BECAUSE I FELT SO FAT!

HA, HA! I SPENT SO LONG PREPARING A ROMANTIC SPEECH THAT I STARTED SOBBING HYSTERICALLY WHEN I TRIED TO GIVE IT AND THEN BROKE UP WITH MY BOYFRIEND BECAUSE HE COULDN'T GUESS WHAT WAS WRONG!

ATTENTION MEN OF THE WORLD: GET YOUR BUS TICKETS OUT OF TOWN WHILE YOU STILL HAVE A CHANCE.

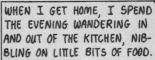

AT THE OFFICE, I'M TOUGH! ENERGIZED! DYNAMIC! DECISIVE! EFFICIENT! IN CONTROL!

WHEN I GET HOME, I SPEND THE EVENING WANDERING IN AND OUT OF THE KITCHEN, NIBBLING ON LITTLE BITS OF FOOD.

WHAT HAPPENS ON THE FREEWAY THAT TRANSFORMS ME FROM SUPERWOMAN TO MINNIE MOUSE?

I'LL GET UP EARLY TOMORROW AND WORK ON THIS REPORT.... I'LL GET UP REALLY EARLY AND GO TO THE HEALTH CLUB BEFORE I WORK ON THIS REPORT....

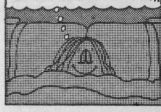

I'LL GET UP REALLY, REALLY EARLY AND PAY BILLS BEFORE I GO TO THE HEALTH CLUB.... I'LL GET UP EXTREMELY EARLY AND DO THE LAUNDRY BEFORE I PAY BILLS BEFORE I GO TO THE HEALTH CLUB BEFORE I WORK ON THAT REPORT.....

AACK! 7:00!! I WAS SUPPOSED TO BE UP AT 3:15!! I'M FINISHED! I'M RUINED! AAACK!!

BRIIING!!

NOT MANY PEOPLE COULD FALL A WHOLE WEEK BEHIND BY WAKING UP AT THEIR NORMAL TIME.

I CAN'T BUY THESE RELATION-SHIP BOOKS. THE SALESCLERK WILL THINK I'M HAVING PROBLEMS WITH MY BOYFRIEND.

WOMEN'S STUDIES

MEN'S STUDIES

CATHY, EVERYONE YOU KNOW KNOWS YOU'RE HAVING PROBLEMS WITH YOUR BOYFRIEND.

WOMEN'S STUDI

ALL YOUR FRIENDS KNOW. ALL MY FRIENDS KNOW. YOUR PARENTS KNOW. YOUR BOYFRIEND KNOWS.... WHAT DO YOU CARE IF SOME SALESCLERK YOU NEVER MET KNOWS ??

IT'S HARD TO LOSE THE ONE PERSON LEFT IN THE WORLD WHO MIGHT THINK I'M DOING BRILLIANTLY.

THERE'S NOTHING WRONG WITH GETTING A FEW POINTERS ON HOW TO FLIRT AND BE ENTICING TO A MAN, CATHY.

THINK ABOUT IT! IF YOU PUT THE SAME EFFORT INTO PERFECTING YOUR RELATIONSHIP SKILLS THAT YOU PUT INTO YOUR CAREER, LOOK AT WHAT YOU'D HAVE!!

MASS HYSTERIA, 7,000 SCRAPS OF PAPER AND A DEAD PLANT.

OK, FINE. LET'S NOT USE YOUR DESK AS AN EXAMPLE.

ON MONDAY, IRVING HAD A HUGE FIGHT WITH HIS BOSS. I COULDN'T HIT HIM WITH MY BIG RELATIONSHIP DISCUSSION.

ON TUESDAY, HE HAD A CLIENT CRISIS. I COULDN'T MAKE HIM TRY TO DEAL WITH OUR PROBLEMS, TOO... TODAY HE HAS A SORE THROAT AND CAR TROUBLE. I JUST CAN'T BRING IT UP.

CATHY, DON'T YOU SEE WHAT YOU'RE DOING??

I'M DOING WHAT ANY SENSITIVE, CARING WOMAN WOULD DO, CHARLENE.

I'M WAITING FOR HIM TO HAVE A PERFECT DAY SO I CAN RUIN IT.

"AN ANSWERING MACHINE PROGRAMMED WITH A CONFIDENT AND VIVACIOUS MESSAGE IS A GREAT WAY TO INSTILL THAT EXTRA BIT OF DESIRE IN A MAN."

"SOUND UNAVAILABLE AND UNATTAINABLE ON YOUR RECORDING, AND YOU UNLEASH THE FULL POWER OF A MAN'S IMAGINATION, DRIVING HIM WILD FOR A CHANCE TO SEE YOU AGAIN."

((RING))

YES!!

"TO ATTAIN BEST RESULTS, YOU MAY HAVE TO ACTUALLY LEAVE THE HOUSE NOW AND THEN...."

SOME CALL IT "THE NEW TRA-
DITIONALISM." SOME CALL IT
"RETROFEMINISM." SOME CALL
IT A BAD JOKE.

WHATEVER THE LABEL, MANY
WOMEN WHO POSTPONED MAR-
RIAGE FOR CAREERS ARE NOW
TRYING TO REDISCOVER THE
DELICATE, FEMININE ART OF
WOOING A MAN'S HEART.

CAN A GENERATION DEVOTED TO
RAISING WOMEN'S SELF-ESTEEM
REALLY REVERT TO HELPLESS
GIGGLES AND DEMURE LITTLE
BLUSHES? ONLY TIME WILL TELL.

HELLO. I WANT TO
HAVE YOUR BABY.

MEANWHILE, BOOK
SALES ARE UP.

THE WINTER COATS
ARE PUT AWAY...

THE HEAVY WOOLS
ARE CAST ASIDE...

THE DYNAMIC WOMAN BURSTS
INTO APRIL WITH A LOOK, A
FLAIR, A FEELING ALL HER OWN..

I HAVEN'T HAD
TIME TO GO
SHOPPING YET.

ONE OF OUR FASHION "MUSTS" FOR SPRING COMES FROM THE MEN'S WORLD: THE VEST!

I THOUGHT WE DIDN'T WANT TO DRESS LIKE MEN.

WE DON'T. MEN BUY ONE BORING VEST AND WEAR IT THEIR WHOLE LIVES.

WOMEN'S VESTS COME IN WILD PRINTS AND BROCADES, GUARANTEEING THAT YOU NOT ONLY NEED TO BUY ONE PER OUTFIT, BUT THEY'LL ALL LOOK RIDICULOUS BY THE FOURTH OF JULY!!

IN THE WORLD OF FASHION, WOMEN ALWAYS MAINTAIN OUR OWN STYLE.

BANKRUPTCY.

ATTENTION ALL EMPLOYEES: I KNOW YOU'RE ALL MUCH TOO BUSY TO SHOP FOR MY SEC- RETARIES WEEK GIFT, SO I'M RAISING MONEY TO BUY MY OWN LITTLE PRESENT.

WHAT AM I BID FOR THE PHOTO NEGATIVES OF MR. PINKLEY AT THE OFFICE CHRISTMAS PARTY?... THE TRANSCRIPT OF CATHY'S LAST PERSONAL CALL TO IRVING?... CONFIDENTIAL SALARY INFORMATION ON THE MANAGEMENT SQUAD?...

... MY SECRET VIDEO, ENTITLED "AFFAIRS IN THE COPIER ROOM", VOLUMES I, II, III, AND....

IT'S INCREDIBLE HOW THEY ALL RALLY WHEN IT'S FOR A PROJECT THEY BELIEVE IN.

INCREDIBLE NEW DRESS, BUT I DIDN'T FIND SHOES TO GO WITH IT YET...

PERFECT SHOES, BUT NO MATCHING SKIRT...WONDERFUL SKIRT, BUT NO MATCHING BLOUSE... GREAT BLOUSE, BUT NO MATCHING PANTS...

FABULOUS JACKET, BUT NO MATCHING SKIRT, PANTS, DRESS SHOES, JEWELRY OR BELT....

THE INDIVIDUAL PARTS OF ME ARE ALL PREPARED TO COME TO WORK, MR. PINKLEY, BUT AS A GROUP WE WON'T BE ABLE TO MAKE IT.

ISOMETRIC EXERCISES TO DO IN THE CAR SO I DON'T GET ANTSY AND EAT MY LUNCH ON THE WAY TO WORK...

MOTIVATIONAL TAPES SO I DON'T GET BORED AND EAT MY LUNCH ON THE WAY TO WORK...

SOOTHING ENVIRONMENTAL TAPES AND STEAMY LOVE STORY TAPES SO I DON'T GET ANNOYED AND EAT MY LUNCH ON THE WAY TO WORK...

DID YOU BRING YOUR LUNCH TODAY, CATHY?

DIDN'T EVEN MAKE IT OUT OF THE DRIVEWAY.

I SPENT HALF AN HOUR TRYING TO DECIDE WHICH FIVE-MINUTE MICROWAVE MEAL TO BUY FOR DINNER...

I SPENT TWO HOURS TRYING TO FIGURE OUT HOW TO TAPE A 30-MINUTE PROGRAM SO I COULD WATCH IT LATER WHEN I'D HAVE MORE TIME...

I THEN DROVE 40 MINUTES ROUND TRIP TO MY HEALTH CLUB SO I COULD WAIT IN LINE FOR 20 MINUTES TO RIDE A STATIONARY BIKE FOR 10 MINUTES...

ANOTHER EVENING WIPED OUT BY MODERN CONVENIENCES.

"THE PROPER DIET SHOULD DERIVE NO MORE THAN 30% OF ITS TOTAL CALORIES FROM FAT, WHICH SHOULD BE EQUALLY DISTRIBUTED AMONG POLYUNSATURATED, MONOUNSATURATED AND SATURATED FAT..."

"IN A 1500-CALORIE DIET, THIS WOULD BE A MAXIMUM OF 50 GRAMS OF FAT, OR 10 GRAMS MORE OR LESS FOR EACH 300-CALORIE INCREASE OR DECREASE IN TOTAL CALORIC ALLOTMENT, FIGURING 9 CALORIES PER GRAM OF FAT, AND 28 GRAMS PER OUNCE..."

"AS IN ALL DIETS, SIMPLE COMMON SENSE SHOULD BE YOUR BEST GUIDE."

I WEIGH TWO POUNDS LESS IF THE SCALE IS ON A CARPETED FLOOR.

THE WORKOUT VIDEO IS IN MY HAND. THE VCR IS 12 INCHES AWAY. PUT THE TAPE IN THE MACHINE. JUST MOVE ONE MUSCLE AND PUT THE TAPE IN THE MACHINE. JUST MOVE. MOVE ANY MUSCLE. JUST MOVE ONE MUSCLE.

THERE'S HALF A CANDY BAR IN THE LEFT POCKET OF A JACKET THAT FELL BEHIND A FILE CABINET, UP TWO FLIGHTS OF STAIRS, 20 MILES AWAY AT THE OFFICE.

BODY POWDER?
LOTION?
OIL?
CREME?
MOUSSE?
GEL?
SPRAY?
TEAL SHADOW?
APRICOT?
TERRA-COTTA?
CHARCOAL?
HAIR UP?
HAIR DOWN?
HAIR BACK?
HAIR CURLED?

SHORT SKIRT?
LONG SKIRT?
MEDIUM SKIRT?
STRAIGHT SKIRT?
FLARED SKIRT?
CAMISOLE?
BLOUSE?
SHORT JACKET?
LONG JACKET?
DRESS?
NUDE HOSE?
OPAQUE HOSE?
SUPPORT HOSE?
NO HOSE?
PANTS?

PUMPS?
FLATS?
OPEN HEEL?
OPEN TOE?
WEDGE?
BELT?
SCARF?
NECKLACE?
BIG EARRINGS?
LITTLE EARRINGS?
PIN?
NAIL POLISH?
HAT?
HUGE PURSE?
TEENSY PURSE?

I WON'T BE IN TO WORK, MR. PINKLEY. I'VE ALREADY USED UP ALL MY DECISION-MAKING SKILLS FOR THE DAY.

IT'S DEPRESSING TO REALIZE WHAT AGE I AM UNTIL I REMEMBER WHAT AGE I'LL BE IN JUST A FEW YEARS...

...JUST LIKE IT'S HORRIBLE TO THINK IT'S AUGUST UNTIL I REMEMBER IT WILL BE CHRISTMAS IN JUST A FEW MONTHS.

IF WE TAKE TIME TO LOOK, LIFE ALWAYS OFFERS A REASSURING PARALLEL FOR US TO CLING TO.

I'M NOT OLD. I'M PRE-HOLIDAY.